contents

What You Need to Know Before Purchasing an Alarm Security System to Protect Your Family & Assets

What is a Burglar Alarm Monitoring System?

A burglar alarm utilizes sensors to monitor, detect, and deter unauthorized entry into a specified environment, such as a home or business. The installation of a security system consists of door sensors, motion detectors, glass-break sensors, and various sensors that instantly trigger detected movement. The purpose of an alarm system is to alert you as the home or business owner and the authorities whenever movement is detected. It could indicate an intrusion, fire, smoke, flood, a dramatic temperature rise, an environmental problem, or a medical crisis.

INDOOR CCTV

SURVEILLANCE CAMERA

LASER SENSORS

MOTION SEN

ALARM PANEL

SECURITY SYSTEMS

CCTV OPERATOR

ROBBERY

SECURITY

SECURITY

LOCKS

How Does a Monitored Burglary System Work?

In the event of a break-in or unauthorized entry, the sensors that trigger the alarm are activated. It could be a door opening, glass shattering, or a motion detector triggered by someone walking in front of it. It sends a signal to the alarm panel, which then alerts the central monitoring station, where a trained operator notifies you of the activity detected.

Simultaneously, the alarm siren serves to scare the intruder away and warn the people in your home or business. If you do not answer the phone, the operator will reach out and inform the people on your emergency call list. They would also dispatch the police, an ambulance, or the fire department depending upon the type of emergency. When you respond, you verify your identity by providing a verbal passcode and whether the situation is a legitimate emergency or a false alarm.

Also available are self-monitoring security systems enabling you to receive alerts directly via text message or e-mail only, instead of a notification call from a live monitoring operator. Not only does a security system monitor, detect and deter, but it also provides peace of mind, knowing that your home, business, family, and valuables are safe.

Why Do You Need a Security System & What are its Benefits?

Equipping yourself with an alarm security system protects your family, pets, assets, and property from burglary or an authorized entry. According to the FBI, an intrusion occurs every 15 seconds in the US alone. More than two million home intrusions are reported every year. One in every five homes experiences home invasion. A home without a security system is three times more likely to be targeted for a break-in than one with a burglar alarm.

Most break-ins - 65% to be precise - occur from 6 a.m. to 6 p.m., not at night. Most likely, they occur when the homeowner is at work, away, or even in the home. Having a family member at home under attack may not deter the intrusion and will be traumatic. An Alarm System provides sufficient warning for the person present to go somewhere safe and take the appropriate action to alert the authorities and get help. Having a security system is vital.

A home security system further protects your family or business from fire, smoke, and carbon monoxide infiltration, a gas that is odorless, colorless, and tasteless. Time is of the essence during a fire, as it only takes seconds for a small flame to ignite into a full-blown fire, causing severe harm to a person or the premises. A security system is designed to call the paramedics to the scene to treat symptoms of Carbon Monoxide poisoning.

Another reason for a home security system is to monitor the activities of an elderly loved one. Some security providers offer medical alert pendants for the elderly, who often live alone. With the press of a button by an elderly person in distress, the authorities or an ambulance can be dispatched to aid them.

An alarm security system is a valuable investment in several ways. According to statistics, the average burglary victim loses $2,400 per break-in; thus, an alarm system can be seen as quite an investment, saving you money in the future. Additionally, having a home or business security system can save up to 15% off an insurance premium. You can save money by using the Smart Home Automation included in some security systems; it is built into a smartphone app to schedule and automate the thermostats and lights, thereby saving electricity.

While leaving town for a business trip or vacation can be nerve-wracking. Installing a home or commercial security system will give you peace of mind, knowing that your premise is secured. Both you and the authorities would be notified in the event of an unauthorized entry. Many security systems allow you to monitor and control your alarm system from the palm of your hand with a phone app or computer. You can arm and disarm your system remotely, check your alarm status and arming log, and monitor the installed cameras for activity. In these busy and tumultuous times, just about everyone can benefit from a good home or business security system.

What are the Main Components of an Alarm Security System?

Before planning and designing the perfect alarm system for your home or business, you must first understand the components and how they work. Below is a glossary that defines the anatomy of an alarm security system with its features and benefits:

Control Panel (the brain of your system)

The alarm's control panel is the system's brain. It may resemble an electrical box or can be built into a numeric keypad. The control panel connects to the other components of your security system, either wired or wireless. It is the element that communicates needed information to a Monitoring Center while it sounds the alarm. Your control panel receives transmissions and signals from alarm sensors. It communicates them back to the monitoring center, thus notifying dispatch operators, who notify you and the authorities. Your control panel includes a backup battery built-in in case of a power outage.

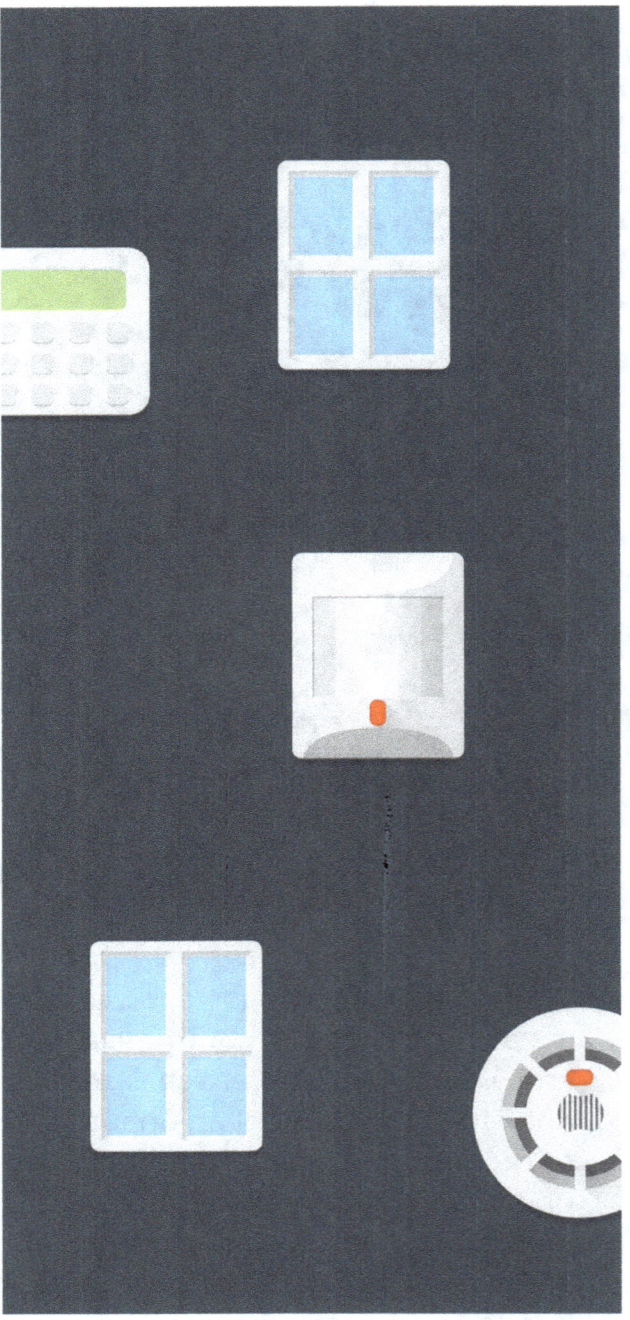

Keypad

The numeric keypad is used to control your alarm system. For instance, when you enter or leave the premises, you press your designated alarm code into a keypad to arm and disarm your system. This keypad indicates whether your system is armed or disarmed and alerts you if a door or window is open. Keypads also make any needed programming changes to your system. They are often installed near the entrance or exit of a home or business.

Door Sensors

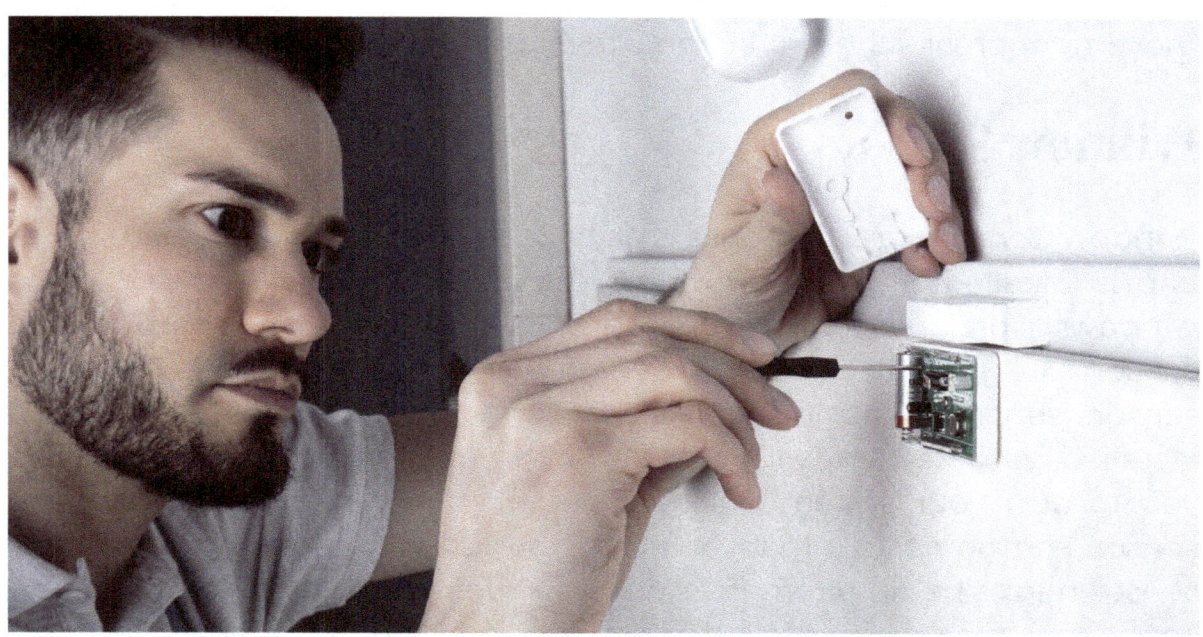

Door sensors have two adjoining magnetic parts. One is installed on the door, and the other is placed on the door frame. When a door is closed, the two components of the sensors are joined together. Only when a door opens will these sensors separate, causing the alarm to sound. Doors are the most common entry point for intruders infiltrating a home or business. When designing an alarm system for your home or business, installing a door sensor on all doors that lead to the outside is imperative. With a door sensor installed, your keypad will notify you if you have left your door open and not allow you to arm your system—unless you close the door or bypass the sensor. If you enable a specific setting, your keypad will chime when a door is opened, letting you know someone has entered.

SECURITY CAMERA   SMOKE DETECTOR   MOTION SENSOR   ALARM SYSTEM

DOOR CONTACT   ALARM SIREN   GLASS BREAK DETECTOR

Garage Door Sensors

It is imperative to monitor the garage door continually, as this is a vulnerable space inside a home or business. A garage door sensor or contact will notify you if your garage door is opened. It comprises a specialized magnetic switch and magnet installed on a garage door constructed to be tough enough to handle harsh environments compared to a regular door sensor. When the garage door is raised, the movement breaks the circuit and activates the alarm.

Window Sensors

Window sensors are comprised of two adjacent magnetic parts. One part is installed on the window, while the other part is installed on the windowsill or frame. When a window is closed, the two parts of the sensors are joined together; only when a window is opened will the sensors separate, causing your alarm to sound. With a window sensor installed, your keypad will notify you of an open window and not allow you to arm your system unless you close the window or bypass the sensor. For rooms with many windows, a motion detector or glass break sensor might be an alternative way to lower your one-time installation cost. If you choose that setting, your keypad will chime when a window is opened.

Motion Sensors

The most common type of motion sensor is an infrared sensor, which identifies the presence of a human body on the premises by detecting body heat and a change in energy. The radius and range for a motion sensor vary depending upon the type of sensor, but a typical motion sensor covers a 90-degree radius and 40 feet across a room. Many motion detectors are designed with a pet immunity feature to avoid being triggered by the presence of rats and small pets up to 70 pounds.

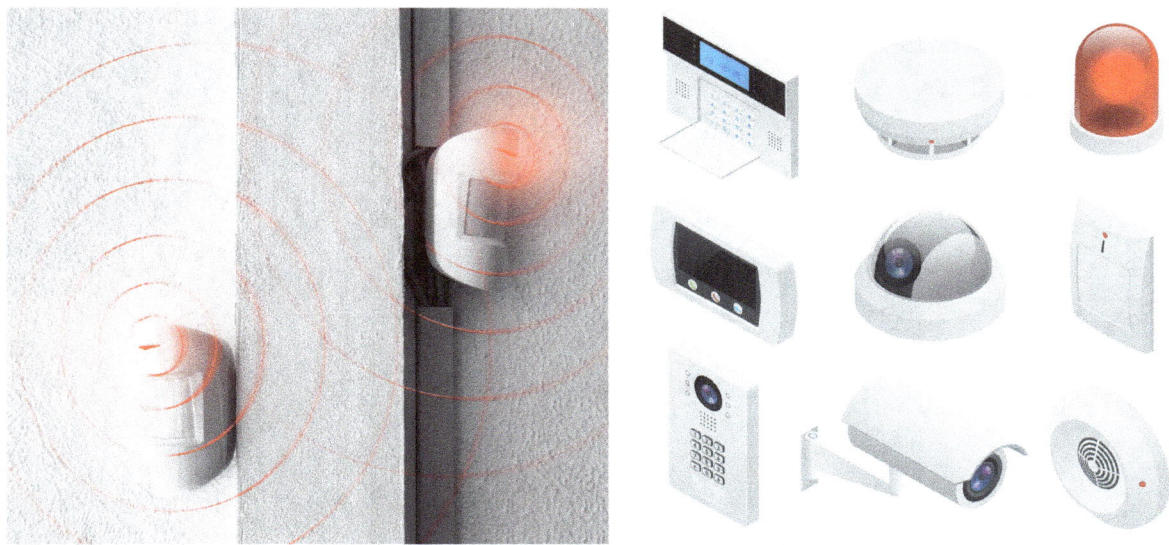

Glassbreak Sensors

 A standard window sensor will alert you only if a burglar slides a window open, so you may need a way to trigger the system if someone shatters your glass without sliding your window open When a glass break detector senses the breaking of glass, it sets off the alarm immediately. It typically detects glass breaking from 25 feet away. A glass break detector provides an extra layer of perimeter protection as a siren would sound immediately after the glass is shattered while the intruder is still standing outside your house or business, allowing more time for authorities to arrive and intervene.

Shock Sensors

Shock sensors provide early detection by sensing vibrations and any sudden forceful impact on a window or door. They detect the shockwaves associated with breaking glass or forced pounding to break down a door. A shock sensor can be installed on a window, stationary glass opening, and a sliding door, where you would not anticipate someone to knock. Shock sensors should not be installed on front doors, where knocking is expected. The downside of installing a shock sensor is that it is more prone to provoke a false alarm elicited by a vibration, not caused by an intruder. For this reason, some may prefer a door, window, or glass break sensor instead. However, shock sensor technology has improved over the years and is no longer prone to provoke false alarms as it once did.

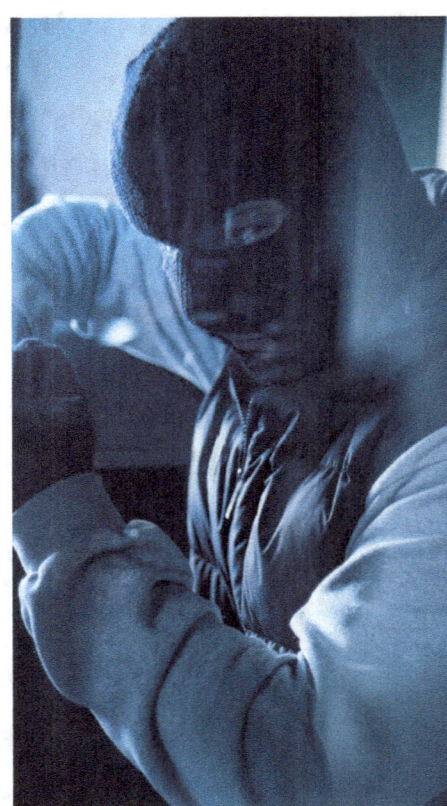

Siren

Sirens release a loud audible signal in the event of your alarm tripping. This signal warns you and the people in the area of the danger at hand and provides the opportunity to flee from an intruder. There are indoor sirens and outdoor sirens. Some sirens have sound-specific alerts specifying the type of emergency, such as a fire or an intruder.

Cellular Alarm Communicators

If a security company is monitoring your alarm system, your system must have a point of communication shared with the security provider's monitoring center to alert them in the event your system goes off. The cellular alarm communicators empower the alarm panel to communicate to your security company's monitoring center via a cellular like cell phones. Some users still utilize the traditional method of communication to a monitoring center via a landline and install this cell guard as a backup—one accessed only after a landline failure.

Panic Button

A panic button can be mounted under a cash register in a business, on a nightstand by your bed, or worn around your wrist or neck. When both buttons are pressed simultaneously for two seconds, it immediately calls for help to your security monitoring center to dispatch police, fire, or medical services. You can program your panic button to activate (sound) a siren. Panic buttons are typically installed in an easily-accessed area that is somewhat hidden, so the intruder will not see the button pressed.

Backup Battery

While an alarm system is powered by a transformer plugged into an outlet, it can still operate in the event of a power outage by switching to a backup battery that lasts between a few to 24 hours. After the power outage, the backup battery automatically recharges when the power is back on. If your backup battery is low or runs out of juice, your keypad or monitoring alarm company will notify you.

2-Way Voice

The two-way audio feature allows a live operator working from a monitoring center to communicate with you via your keypad's intercom in an emergency. This comes in handy when you do not have your phone with you and will also help reduce false alarms, as you can advise the operator not to dispatch help in the event of a false signal.

Modes to Arm Your Alarm System: Armed Away vs. Armed Stay & Entry / Exit Delays

Alarm systems typically have two modes of arming; armed away and armed stay. Armed Away is the mode to select when leaving your home or business as it activates all sensors. Armed Stay is the mode you select when you want to arm your system but remain inside your home or business. It allows you to walk about freely, as it activates all sensors except for the motion detectors. Armed stay is a suitable mode when we are sleeping or working late and need to walk around the premises.

Both arming modes allow an entry and exit delay for the specific sensors selected when you come in and out. For example, you may need to program a 30, 60, or 90-second delay from the moment the system is armed from the keypad till you exit through the front door. When you arm your system, your keypad will beep to remind you that there is a certain amount of time to exit. Alternatively, when coming into your home or business from your door you selected for delay, your keypad will beep, indicating a certain amount of time to walk over to your keypad and disarm your system - or else your alarm will go off.

There are lesser-used arming modes. Instant Arming is the same as Armed Stay but does not allow for an entry or exit delay. You use this mode when not expecting anyone to enter or exit. Maximum mode is the same as Armed Away but does not provide a delayed entry or exit.

You can arm and disarm your premises from the keypad, a mobile app, or key fob. You may choose to customize the auto arm for a specific time. When arming your system, all doors and windows with sensors need to be closed. If one is left open, your keypad will prompt you to close the particular door or window or bypass that sensor in order to arm your system.

Third-Party Guard Patrol Car Dispatch & its Benefits

Some alarm monitoring providers offer the option of dispatching an on-site security patrol car with a two-way radio for direct communication to your monitoring center should your alarm be triggered. The patrol car would physically verify if the police, the fire department, or an ambulance should be dispatched. This third-party security will patrol the exterior and interior of your property if desired. A third-party patrol car helps deter those not allowed on your property, such as loiterers or the homeless.

There are benefits to opting for third-party patrol services. Some police stations choose not to respond to an alarm trigger unless verified by video verification, a service alarm monitoring providers may offer by logging on to your cameras to verify if it is a real emergency or a false alarm. Another requirement to dispatch the police is for the third-party patrol car to verify an emergency because about 95% of alarm triggers are false alarms. Once on your premises, the third-party patrol car would contact the police to verify the emergency.

If you live in an area where police respond to unverified alarm triggers, you may still experience a delayed response as verified alarms get priority. You may experience a delay if the police are busy dealing with another issue. An additional benefit of dispatching a third-party patrol service car is that it helps reduce false alarm fines by your city since they waste city dollars and the police's time.

Life Safety Devices

According to the NFPA, a fire occurs in the US every 24-seconds, while nationwide, a fire death occurs every 144 minutes. Thirty-five percent of the smoking fire fatalities had been sleeping, and 17 percent could not act. You are more likely to have a life safety event than a break-in. Emergency sensors provide your system with a crucial added layer of security. Emergency sensors can save the lives of your loved ones. They range from smoke detectors and heat detectors to carbon monoxide detectors, water flood sensors, and low/ high probe temperature probe sensors. Fire codes typically require local smoke alarms to sound in the event of a fire in your home but having a monitored smoke alarm goes a step further by not only sounding a siren but calling for help as well.

Below is a glossary that defines the anatomy of life safety devices with their features and benefits:

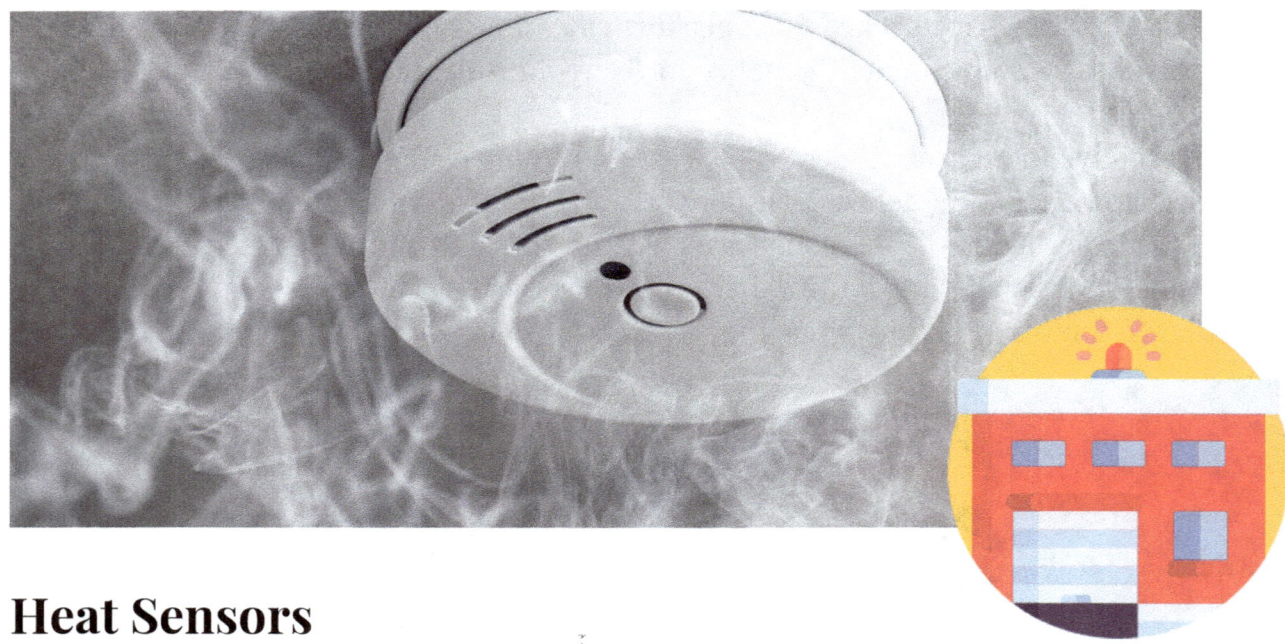

Heat Sensors

Heat detectors sense heat from a fire and signal your alarm to alert you. A fire normally causes a quick rise in temperature in the vicinity of its occurrence. Heat detectors can either go off when detecting high temperatures, often when the temperature reaches 135°F or greater, or when it detects your temperature rising at an unusually rapid rate. Heat detectors are typically installed in areas where you expect smoke or dust, like kitchens, basements, furnace and laundry rooms, hallways, stairways, garages, attics, and fireplaces.

Smoke Detectors

Smothering or slow-burning fires can sometimes generate little heat, making it difficult to detect via heat detectors. Smoke detectors are activated when they detect smoke and may release an audible alert earlier in the development of a fire. In some cases, smoke detectors are recommended over heat detectors since they can detect a fire before heat detectors can. However, if the alarm's coverage space accumulates dust, this can elicit false alarms; therefore, heat detectors might be a better fit for some people. Smoke detectors can also be triggered by burnt food and steam, so they are not always recommended for installation in a kitchen or a room where people smoke. However, the technology for smoke detectors has improved over the years, enhancing the fault detection of cooking alarms.

Carbon Monoxide Sensors

Carbon monoxide is known as the silent killer as an odorless, colorless, tasteless gas that kills 400 people and hospitalizes 50,000 people annually. Carbon monoxide detectors indicate the presence of this toxic gas, one difficult to determine without a carbon monoxide detector in your home if you have even one gas appliance. More advanced modes digitally display the level of carbon monoxide or even read it aloud. Carbon monoxide detectors do not detect smoke or explosive gasses: only carbon monoxide gas that can cause positioning.

Many security providers now offer a combination 3-in-1 smoke, heat, and carbon monoxide detector in one device that detects and alerts with rising temperature, elevated smoke, and carbon monoxide detection. New devices often include a LED light that indicates the type of emergency; some have a "one go, all go" feature, where if one device goes off, all devices go off, so you hear them in case you are in a different room. It can be a good idea to install life safety devices on each floor, so if your device in the basement goes off, a device in your second-floor bedroom will go off, increasing the chances of hearing it.

Flood Sensors

Flood detectors can be installed in areas prone to water leakage; for instance, under a sink, where there are pipes, or around the pan of your water heater since they detect the presence of water and moisture. Flood Sensors notify you early in the event of water damage caused by leaking or burst pipes in water heaters, HVAC units, washers, etc. In turn, it prevents costly damage from mold and mildew on floors and walls or the ceiling falling in, thus minimizing loss. With flood detectors, you are typically notified by your security company and receive a text notification, but the police are generally not dispatched.

Low/High-Temperature Sensors

Temperature sensors accurately measure temperatures inside a building. You will be notified if the temperature goes above or below pre-set standards. Low/high-temperature probes can be installed in freezers to notify you before the pipes freeze or in wine cellars if your wine cellar is too warm. They can be installed anywhere in need of proper temperature maintenance. Like flood sensors, you would typically be notified without police being dispatched.

How does an Alarm System Communicate to a Monitoring Center?

Much like many forms of communication technology, the way alarm systems communicate with monitoring centers has changed considerably over the years. The traditional method has been via a landline, similar to how a fax machine communicates. The alarm system overtakes your phone line and dials the monitoring station.

There is no need to reserve a dedicated phone line for your burglar alarm system, as your alarm system would only dial into your landline if your alarm system goes off.

Most burglar alarm systems today no longer communicate via landline but via cellular alarm communicators that allow an alarm panel to communicate with a monitoring center, like how cell phones communicate. Some users still use the traditional method of communication via landline and rely on a cellular connection as a backup device accessed after a landline failure.

Cellular alarm communicators, or cell guards, for short, generally transmit signals faster than a landline. The use of burglar alarm systems communicating with a cell guard instead of a landline has dramatically increased since many people are no longer using landlines in their homes and businesses.

Another reason there are more systems with cell guards' vs. landlines is that landlines can be cut, and harsh winds can disrupt landline service, preventing the transmission of signals to a monitoring center. With a cellular alarm connection, a security system could function even during a power outage. Users no longer must rely on a landline to transmit signals, as many security companies now offer systems without needing landlines, whether monitored professionally or self-monitored. In other words, you no longer need a phone call to instigate a "call for help!"

What is the Difference between a Hardwired Alarm System vs. a Wireless Security Alarm System? What are the advantages and Disadvantages of Each, and Which Should I Choose?

Security system providers include wired and wireless alarm systems in their product lines. The main difference is the cabling or wiring element. A wired system requires each sensor to be wired to a control panel (the system's brain). A wireless alarm system uses a short-range radio transmitter to communicate, and each sensor is connected wirelessly—virtually eliminating the need for wiring. All your door, window, motion, and glass-break sensors would be wireless and battery operated. Unlike the sensors, your keypad and control panel might need to be hardwired to an outlet for power. Sometimes the control panel and keypad are one unit instead of two.

Both hardwired and wireless alarm systems come with their share of advantages and disadvantages. A hardwired system's advantage is that it is considered more reliable than wireless systems, as they do not communicate wirelessly via radio waves with much less chance of inference. Wired alarm systems can be less prone to false alarms because they do not rely on radio waves. A wired system would generally require less maintenance than a wireless one since you would not have to change batteries or deal with communication issues.

However, there are a few disadvantages to installing a hardwired system. A wired security system may not physically access all areas of your home or business if you cannot run wires to that location, or you may end up with exposed wires. Another disadvantage is the additional time and labor needed since you must run wires for each sensor. More time and labor will mean a more expensive one-time setup fee. Another disadvantage of installing a hardwired alarm system is that sometimes it may be challenging to add wired sensors in the future in the event of a home or business expansion. Plus, a wired system is vulnerable to the dangers of line cutting by intruders invading the property.

However, there are a few disadvantages to installing a hardwired system. A wired security system may not physically access all areas of your home or business if you cannot run wires to that location, or you may end up with exposed wires. Another disadvantage is the additional time and labor needed since you must run wires for each sensor. More time and labor will mean a more expensive one-time setup fee. Another disadvantage of installing a hardwired alarm system is that sometimes it may be challenging to add wired sensors in the future in the event of a home or business expansion. Plus, a wired system is vulnerable to the dangers of line cutting by intruders invading the property.

A hardwired alarm system can be a good option for those in the process of building a home or business since you can run the alarm wires before erecting the walls. A hardwired system is also a good option if you move into a space that already has alarm wires to utilize.

Wireless alarm systems have their advantages and disadvantages. The advantage of a wireless burglar alarm system is the ease of setting up and installing - and usually less expensive. The system will be even less expensive if you purchase a DIY(Do-it-yourself) wireless system. You can take the wireless system and sensors with you when you move. A wireless system can sometimes reach more areas than its wired counterpart since you do not have to run wires. Now that wireless sensors are encrypted, they are almost as secure as a wired system. As a bonus, they do not include wires that could potentially be cut.

The disadvantage of installing a wireless alarm system is that they communicate via radio waves, meaning that each component and sensor must operate within a range of the central station. For large homes and businesses, a wireless system may not be ideal as it would leave certain areas unsecured and unable to communicate with the central panel. A wireless system also requires batteries for each sensor, which last 2 to 7 years, depending upon the amount of use, and they will eventually need to be changed.

A wireless system makes sense if you are frequently mobile or cost-conscious. Roughly 90% of the new systems are wireless due to their improved functionality and easy installation. A hybrid system is a wired security system with wireless sensors added through a wireless receiver.

What is the Difference between a Monitored Alarm System Vs. a Self-Monitored Alarm Security System?

The main difference between a monitored alarm system and a non-monitored security system is the duration of events that occur during your alarm going off. In the event of a break-in, both systems would sound their siren; however, with a monitored alarm system, a live 24/7 professional monitoring operator notifies you and the authorities if an alarm is tripped. Before contacting the authorities, the agent would first call to verify that it is not a false alarm since they happen frequently. The alarm agent would then let you know what caused the alarm to go off. For example, they might say your back door, or some front motion triggered it.

If you do not answer the phone, the operator will call your emergency contact list and ask for your verbal password to verify your identity. A live operator is always ready to respond with a monitored burglar alarm system. A monitored system is generally more costly than an unmonitored security system and comes with a monthly monitoring fee. Generally, with a monitored alarm system, a personal installer designs and installs the alarm system and sensors.

With unmonitored security systems, the system does not automatically contact a central monitoring station. Instead, you would be notified of an alarm trigger via text message, phone app, and e-mail. You would call the authorities for help instead of receiving a call from a live agent. This option might work for those confident they can respond to text messages and e-mails quickly and consistently. However, if you are asleep, at work, or in a meeting, you might miss an important call that signals endangerment in your home or business!

Your siren would still sound in the event of your alarm to scare the intruder away and warn people in the surrounding area. With an unmonitored security system, you would lose that extra layer of security and speed of action that makes a significant difference for you and your family or business. A self-monitored security system is generally cheaper, and in most cases, you design the system and install the alarm sensors yourself. You can purchase a DIY home alarm security system (Do-it-Yourself) online or in-store. DIY systems can be monitored or unmonitored.

What You Need to Know Before
Purchasing a Health Medical Alert System

What is a Health Medical Alert Solution?

Medical Alert Systems, also known as Personal Emergency Response Systems, allows you or a loved one to wear a bracelet or pendant with a help button and two-way voice connectivity to a health monitoring center, where a live agent can dispatch police, fire, or ambulance in the event of an emergency, such as a fall or break-in. Family members or neighbors can also be notified. Medical alert systems often come with fall detection, which alerts a live agent when you or your loved ones fall and cannot press the emergency button. On-the-go medical alert systems often have GPS location capability, so first responders and loved ones would know where to find you.

Who Benefits from a Medical Alert System?

With 250,000 people turning 65 every month, a health Medical Alert System allows seniors and people with special needs to maintain their independence by providing them and their loved ones with peace of mind, knowing that help is always there 24/7 with a press of a button. With the proper assistance in a cost-effective manner, it competes favorably with hiring home aid or living in a senior living facility. In an emergency such as a fall or a break-in, not only can the police, fire department, or an ambulance be alerted and dispatched, but loved ones can also be notified. If the issue is minor and no professionals are needed, the live agent can notify a family member or neighbor.

Medical Alert Solutions are great options for seniors who live alone and want to remain independent and continue doing activities they love. It is a great option for those prone to falling and who want to overcome that fear. These systems are also ideal for those with poor health, eyesight, hearing, dementia, disabled or recovering from surgery, and fear they may faint.

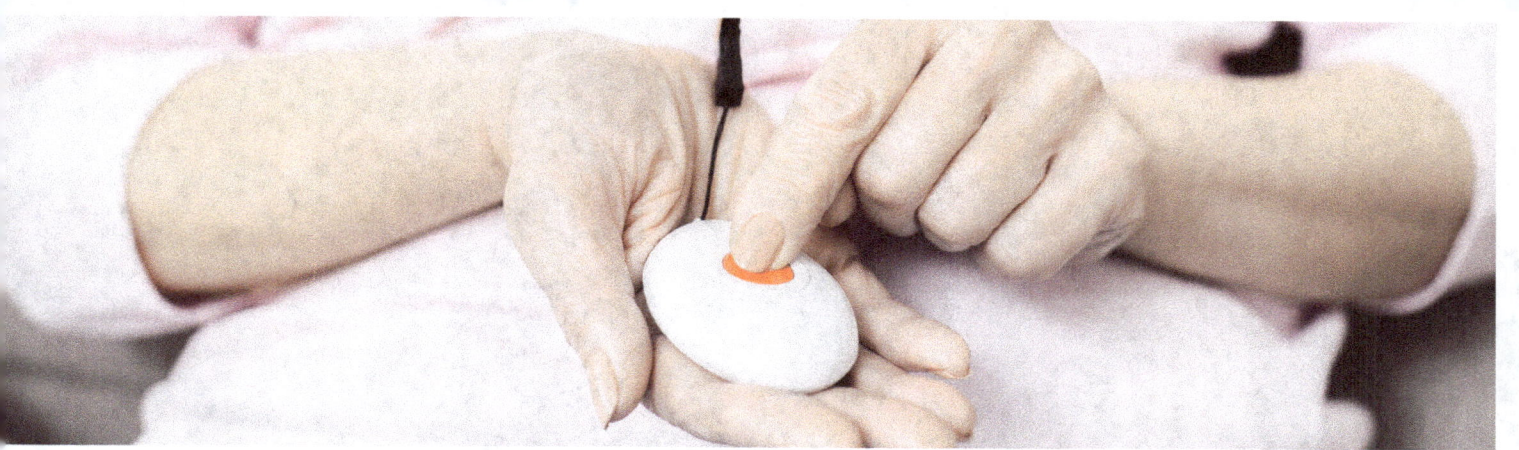

How Does a Medical Alert System Work and How Do I Receive Help?

You or a loved one would wear a bracelet or pendant and push a button when emergency assistance is needed. Pressing the button sends a signal to a live operator in the monitoring center, allowing you or your loved one with the wearable to communicate with a live agent via a two-way speaker. The live operator would assess the situation, send the appropriate emergency first responders - such as the police, fire department, or paramedics - and notify and connect you to your emergency contact list, typically family members and neighbors.

How Do Medical Alert Systems Communicate with Monitoring Centers?

Whereas in the past, medical alert devices communicated to monitoring centers via landlines, confining them to work at home, today, many systems communicate with monitoring centers via cellular networks, allowing these systems to work outside the home with On-the-go Systems. In-Home Alert Systems can communicate to a monitoring center via your landline, VOIP, with some via cellular.

In-Home Systems and Mobile On-the-go Systems

There are typically two types of Medical Alert Systems available: in-home and mobile on-the-go. In-Home Systems come with a base station that plugs into an outlet for power and communicates with a monitoring center via a landline, VOIP, or cellular device. Mobile On-the-go Systems typically come with a mobile base unit & have GPS location capability, so first responders would know where to find you.

Monitored Medical Alert Systems vs. Non-Monitored Alert Systems

A Monitored Medical Alert System sends an alert to a live operator in a monitoring center. It allows for two-way communication, whereas a Non-Monitored Alert System does not alert a live operator. Instead, it notifies an emergency contact person, whether a family member, friend or neighbor. Whereas having a Monitored Alert System is a better solution, providing a second layer of security, it comes with a monthly monitoring fee, while a Non-Monitored Alert System does not.

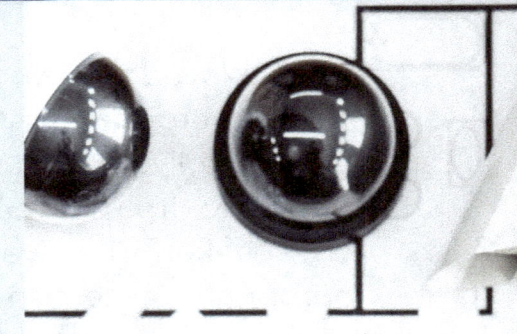

Components of a Health Medical Alert Solution

Medical Alert Bracelet or Wearable:

A small, water-resistant pendant or wristband that can be pressed to alert a live agent when help is needed.

Base Station:

An in-home medical alert system has a base station plugged into a wall outlet for power and a telephone jack to communicate with the monitoring center. Some communicate via VoIP or cellular technology that does need to connect to a phone jack.

Mobile Base Unit:

This allows you to use your pendant inside and outside your home; it uses GPS technology to pinpoint your location for first responders, family, and friends.

Wall-Mounted Buttons:

An emergency button in a set location, whether on a table or nightstand. You or a loved one can walk over to press it in an emergency.

Fall Detection:

Some Medical Alert Solitons come with fall detection, using sensors to detect and register falls automatically, thereby alerting a dispatch center.

Mobile App and Online Portal

A mobile app and online portal allow you to access your account to make any necessary changes to your emergency contact list (to be notified in the event of an emergency) and to set alerts and notifications about your care or the care of your loved ones.

Lockbox

Some Medical Alert Solution providers offer a lockbox that can be easily installed on a doorknob, railing, or fence without tools, thereby allowing family, friends, neighbors, or first responders to gain quick and easy access to the house without the need for forced entry.

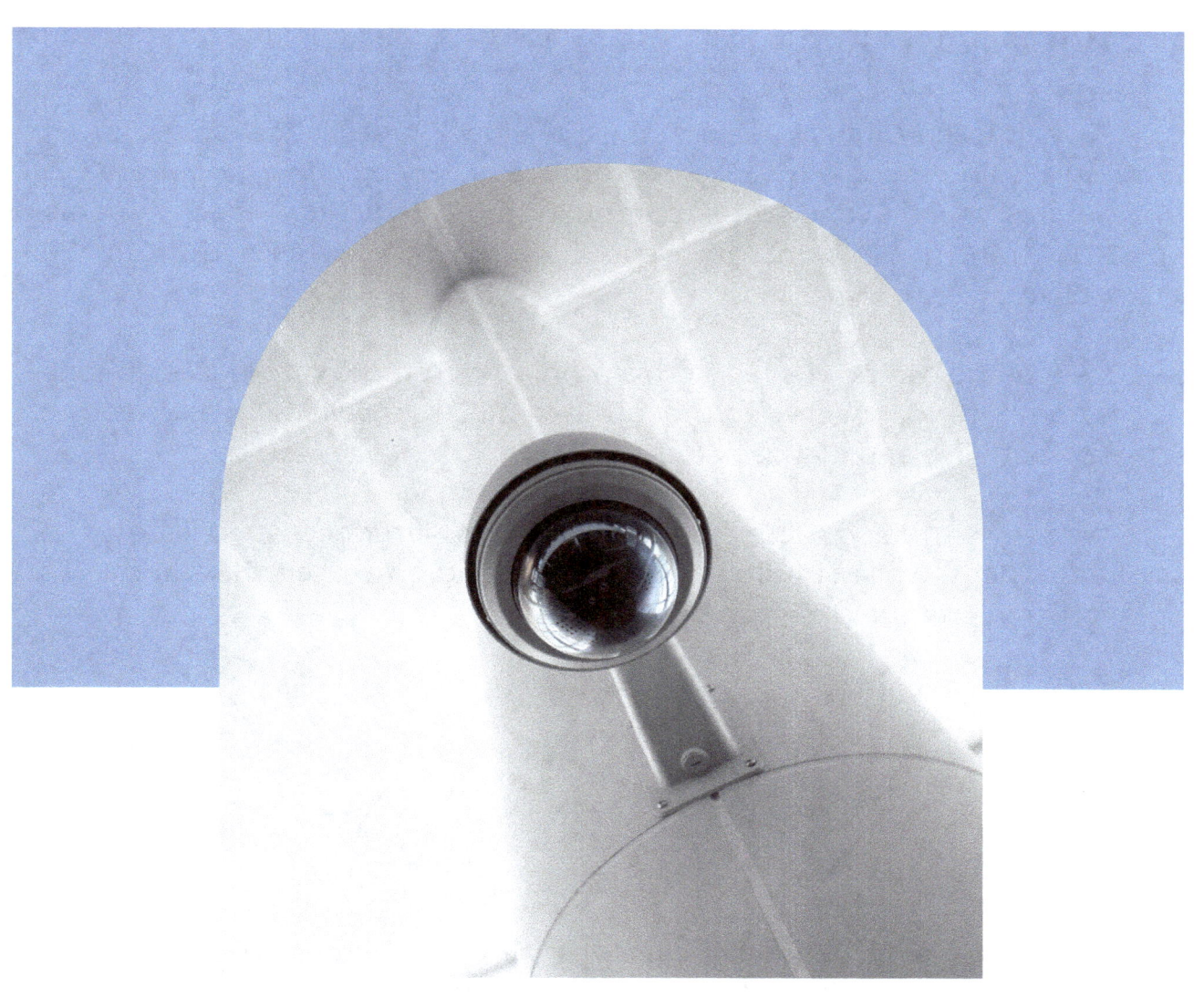

What You Need to Know Before Purchasing a CCTV Surveillance System to Protect Your Family & Assets

What is CCTV?

CCTV (Closed-Circuit Television) is a video surveillance system that displays and records footage of premises and people in a target area to monitor security and deter potential criminals. Using video cameras, CCTV transmits a signal to a specific place to view all activity in the subject area.

The footage can be viewed from a monitor or remotely from a cell phone or computer connected to the internet. CCTV surveillance allows you to view both live and playback footage.

This device helps deter crimes such as littering, vandalism, and harassment, while simultaneously preventing employee theft and even worker idleness, as they are being monitored!

Why Do You Need CCTV?

CCTV surveillance cameras help investigate and deter incidents such as theft, robberies, and unlawful activities. Since your premises are being monitored, criminals often think twice before stealing or committing a crime in the vicinity. In any case, you will have the footage to reveal who has committed the act and the ability to save and transmit it to the authorities. CCTV is especially beneficial in high-crime areas.

In addition to crime prevention, CCTV monitoring helps increase employee productivity and efficiency. Studies show that employees work better when monitored, making CCTV a good investment. You will see that CCTV pays for itself by ensuring more efficient employee habits. CCTV surveillance also provides footage of work accidents for liability and insurance purposes. It further can keep track of the elderly cared for at home and children coming home from school. Some appreciate that it can monitor pets when the owner is away. CCTV, in essence, provides peace of mind.

The Components of a CCTV System

Before you start planning for and designing a CCTV System for your home or business, you must first understand the components of a CCTV System and how they work.

Video Recorder

Most CCTV Surveillance Systems come with a device that records and stores footage, which can be viewed live or played back. A video recorder needs a power supply.

Two Types of Recorders

CCTV recorders take the form of NVR (Network Video Recorders) and DVR (Digital Video Recorders). The difference between NVRs and DVRs is in how they process video data and the types of wiring and cameras found in them.

DVR Systems

A DVR processes video data via an analog signal sent to the recorder. A DVR system is not as structurally complex as an NVR system, given that a DVR system uses analog cameras equipped with coaxial BNC cables. A coaxial cable does not provide power to the camera, so an additional wire is usually included to power the device. Coaxial cables are bulkier than cat5 wires used by NVRs, so installations can be more challenging in tight spaces. A DVR system requires each camera to be hardwired, and it cannot use wireless cameras, unlike an NVR recorder.

NVR Systems

NVR systems incorporate the latest technology to provide more enhanced, improved performance compared to a DVR system and are more structurally complex. NVR encodes and processes the video data in the camera, then streams it to the NVR to be used for storage and remote viewing. An NVR system uses IP cameras (standalone image-capturing devices) and standard Ethernet cables such as cat5 or cat6 wiring to transmit data. NVR system wiring is easier to install and less bulky than DVR wiring. An added benefit of NVR systems is that not every camera needs to be hardwired to the NVR model if connected to the same wireless network. The NVR system requires only one cable to supply video, audio, and power, unlike a DVR system that requires two. A separate mic may need to be purchased for audio recordings in both systems.

Should I choose an NVR System or a DVR System?

Both systems record footage and are reliable options. Whereas in the past, an NVR system offered more than a DVR system, DVR systems have now improved. The main differences between them are cost, the manner of video transmission, and the type of camera in the unit. NVR systems use the latest technology and offer better picture quality and easier installation; however, the cost reflects these enhancements.

I recommend an NVR system in most cases. If your space is pre-wired with coaxial cables, which only work with a DVR system, you may want to purchase a DVR system to avoid needing rewiring.

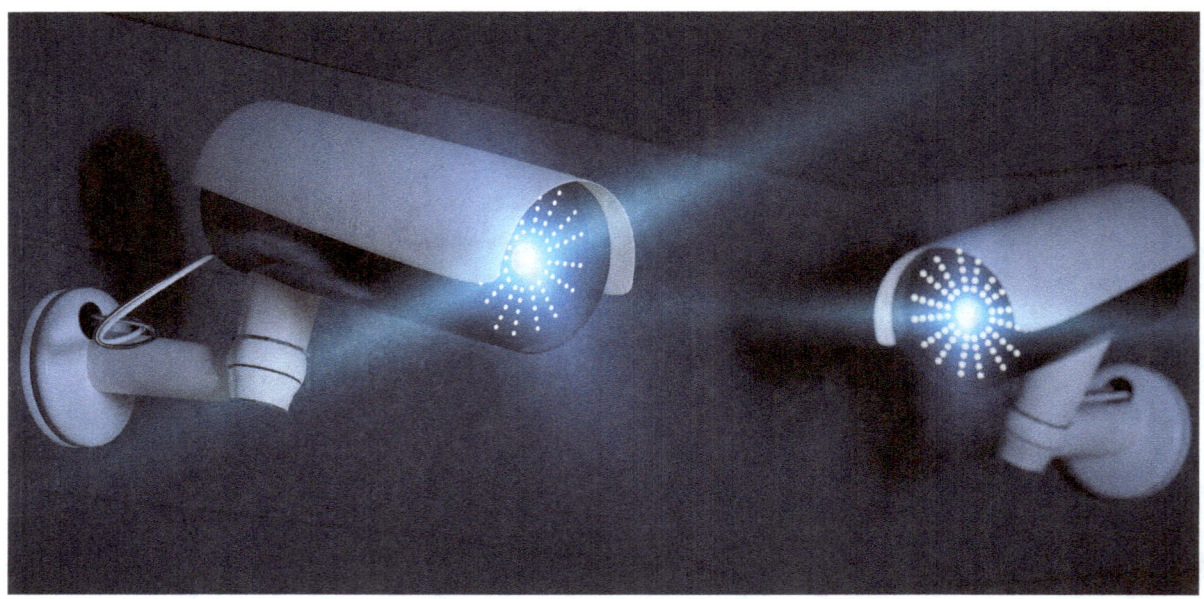

Storage (Hard Drive)

CCTV recorders have a hard drive to record footage. Choosing the right amount of hard drive space will require calculating the video length you need to store and the bitrate and resolution of your camera shots. Suppose you need to record for an exact number of days. In that case, you may want to consider purchasing a cloud-based storage system, which can record for a period of exactly 30, 60, 90 days, or whatever time is needed. It goes straight to the cloud (located online) and can be accessed via a mobile app or online web portal anytime. You can save footage to a USB stick, external hard drive, or your computer.

Cloud Cameras

Cloud-based video hosting takes recorded video footage, compresses it - and often encrypts it - then sends it to a secure off-site server, stored for future access. The footage can be accessed via an online portal or phone app. With a cloud-based system, you would not need an NVR or DVR recorder; sometimes, a small bridge is needed for where the footage records and holds data temporarily before it streams to the cloud overnight—thus preventing slowing your internet connection during the day. Cloud-camera systems reduce the risk of smash and grabs. Cloud-Managed Video Systems allow you to add additional cameras easily in the future since they do not come with a recorder that holds only a certain number of cameras. While cloud cameras require less hardware, they mandate a strong internet connection and can slow down your internet connection. Typically, 2-3 Mbps of upload speed (not download speed) is required for each cloud camera.

Security Cameras

Before you start planning for and designing a CCTV system for your home or business, you need to understand the different varieties of cameras that come with a CCTV system and how they work. A camera is an electronic device that records footage for monitoring and playback purposes. These cameras come in different types, shapes, sizes, styles, configurations, etc. Cameras are designed for indoor and outdoor use, and some are designed for both. Many day/night cameras come with infrared LEDs (night vision), making it possible to monitor the target area even in the dark of night. Many cameras are vandal resistant (containing metal housing), making them difficult to tamper, vandalize, or interfere with. Camera footage typically can be viewed remotely from anywhere worldwide if you connect your system to the internet. Many cameras now record footage in HD, offering high-resolution images from 720p to 4K. The most common type of CCTV cameras are:

Dome Cameras

A dome-shaped casing houses the camera. They tend to be more discreet in appearance, with the camera's shape making it hard for people to identify which direction the camera is facing, rendering the camera a good deterrent with a wider viewing angle.

Bullet Cameras

Bullet cameras, with their cylinder shape, tend to be more visible and less discrete than other cameras. You might want a camera to be visible at times. Bullet cameras are typically better in harsh environments, where dirt accumulates, and their casing protects against sunlight, rain, and glare. They are better for viewing longer distances than dome cameras.

PTZ (Pan, Tilt, and Zoom Cameras)

PTZ cameras allow you to control the camera lens by panning left and right, tilting up and down, and zooming in and out. This is ideal when you want to monitor your CCTV footage live on-site and have blind spots, which you can monitor by tilting and panning the camera.

Wired vs. Wireless Cameras

Wired cameras are hardwired to a recorder, while wireless cameras, on the other hand, do not need to be connected to a recorder. Wireless cameras are easy to install as a result. Since they are wireless, they have a cleaner installation than a hardwired camera that cannot hide its wires behind walls. However, if the wireless camera is not battery operated, it will need to be plugged into an outlet for power. It would still be considered a wireless camera because it does not need to connect to a recorder. Wireless cameras also come with some disadvantages. Wireless cameras that need a dedicated frequency to transmit signals can sometimes be interrupted or interfered with, causing the unit to lose footage. Some wireless cameras do not record continually; instead, they only record motion clips for 30 seconds or a few minutes. Wireless cameras sometimes use a cheaper material and are of lesser quality than hardwired cameras, but it is not always the case.

CCTV Video Analytics & its Benefits

Cameras with video analytics allow you to receive custom notifications for selected events. For example, a camera automatically sends a short clip of a motion-triggered event to your mobile device or email. Cameras can differentiate between people, animals, and vehicles to eliminate sending notification clips of small animals such as cats and dogs or cars passing by. Some cameras have two-way audio, allowing you to warn the intruder.

CCTV systems send useful data to business owners to increase profits and improve operations. Some of the helpful data that CCTV systems can provide a business owner include:

Occupancy Tracking technology alerts you to the number of occupants in your establishment, helping you stay compliant with local regulations and providing a beneficial customer behavioral analysis.

People Counting technology counts the number of people that cross a designated area. Some tracking technology has facial recognition.

Crowd Detection technology detects crowd density by counting the number of people entering your establishment at any given time. It provides valuable information such as your busiest times of the day and if a promotion you are running leads to more traffic.

Queue Monitoring technology alerts you when your line is long or moving slowly while tracking customer wait times. When you get an extended line alert, you can deploy a staff member to prevent sales abandonment due to long lines.

Heat Mapping technology helps track customer movement in a store to inform you which areas are getting the most traction. It comes in an easy-to-read, color-coded graphical report to place your top-selling items in those areas.

Surveillance Camera Mounts & Housings

Before you start planning for and designing a CCTV system for your home or business, you need to understand the different types of camera housings and mounts that come with a CCTV system and their purposes. The camera housing is sometimes necessary, depending upon the environment in which the camera is positioned. For instance, if the temperature varies and weather conditions are humid, rainy, or snowy, the camera housing ensures that the camera is protected from extreme weather conditions. Also, the camera housing can help prevent tampering and vandalism, as it is often made from vandal-proof metal materials. CCTV mounting brackets, which include outdoor camera mounts, wall mounts, and ceiling mounts, help you install and mount CCTV cameras on surfaces where it would be difficult or impossible to install otherwise.

Wires for CCTV – Exposed or Hidden?

Hardwired CCTV cameras require a wire to run from the camera to the recorder; some cameras will also need an extra wire for power. The best way to hide and secure CCTV wires is to run them behind walls. CCTV wires located inside walls are difficult to be tampered with or cut. If your site is still under construction, you can pre-wire before erecting the sheetrock. Businesses with drop ceilings can have their CCTV wiring hidden behind the ceiling. However, more effort and planning would be required in spaces without a drop ceiling. Sometimes, when wires cannot be hidden due to a brick wall or cement, you may need to run some conduit or wire molding to conceal them. CCTV wires can be wired within baseboards that generally take the form of wooden boards across the bottom of walls. Exposed CCTV wires can be painted to blend in with the walls or purchased in a colored variation to match them.

Viewing Footage from your Monitor Locally

CCTV cameras can be viewed from any standalone monitor or a TV if your recorder and monitor/ TV come with the same variety of connectors, whether HDMI or VGA.

Built-in Microphone/Audio

Cameras with audio recording capability are getting more popular of late. Most CCTV cameras are video only and require a microphone or additional feature to enable audio recording. Some CCTV cameras are equipped with an integrated microphone that allows for clear audio recording up to a certain number of feet away from the camera. Some CCTV cameras also include two-way audio capability, allowing you to hear and speak to the person in front of your camera from your phone, wherever you are. You may need to post a voice recording sign to let people know you are recording voices in some settings. Note that the act of recording audio comes with stricter legal limitations as compared to video not recording audio, so check your local ordinances before investing in a microphone or other audio device.

Camera Placements

Before you begin your installation, walk around the areas where you plan to situate your cameras. If possible, stand at each intended location to get a better picture of what images and perspectives the cameras will capture. Generally, what you see from where you are standing is what the camera will see. Pay attention to that perspective and ask, does it allow a generous view? More importantly, does the area you are standing in capture the area you would like covered? If the answer is no, you may need to find another location to mount your camera. When installing hardwired CCTV cameras, you may start by figuring out where you want to station your recorder first and then determine the camera locations. You will get a better idea of the difficulty of the wire run from each camera to the recorder. If installing a wireless camera that requires a power outlet, note how far the wireless camera is from your outlet and whether the wire will be exposed.

Typically, cameras are installed in the corner of the room opposite the entry. This vantage point usually provides the best coverage and captures any intruder on film before they gain access. The best height for a camera stands at the 10-foot level or higher. This is high enough to keep people from accessing the camera unless they use a ladder. Understand that if you aim a camera at a large window or an exterior door, the view may be somewhat limited during bright or sunny days because the sun's glare prevents a clear view. All cameras are equipped with an auto iris, and while they work well, they still have their limits and must adjust to the light level inside or outside. You will want to install cameras near entry points and vulnerable areas of your home or business with safes and valuables.

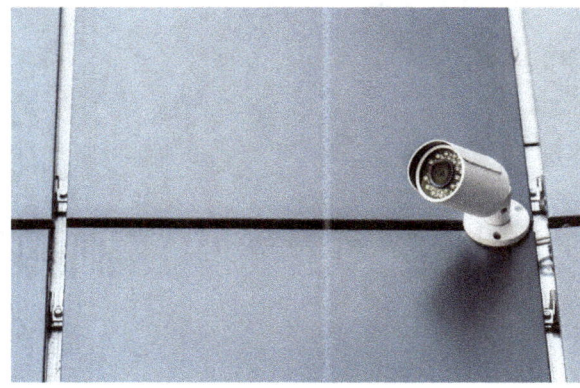 

CCTV Remote Viewing on Phone App & Computer Software

Most CCTV systems come with a phone app and computer software integration for PC and Mac, allowing you to view your camera footage live, as well as playback footage from your cell phone, tablet, or computer remotely while away - from anywhere in the world - if you connect your cameras to your network via Wi-Fi or hardwire it from your recorder to your router. You will receive notifications straight to your phone or email for specific events you choose. You may want your camera to send you a notification or a short clip for every person approaching your front porch. Newer cameras can identify and differentiate between people, animals, cars, etc., so you will not receive notification of a bird or squirrel approaching.

A Few CCTV Features & Benefits

CCTV Resolution

A camera's resolution equals the number of pixels on an image measured vertically and horizontally. The higher the resolution, the clearer an image projects. However, the resolution is not the only factor that affects image quality. Other factors include light performance, frame rate, lens, image sensor, and night vision. The high-definition level generally starts at 1280 x 720 pixels and goes up from there. A high-definition camera can project a clearer image of someone's face or even a license plate number.

Field of View

CCTV's field of view generally ranges from 90 degrees to 140 degrees. The more coverage you need, the higher it needs to be.

Night Vision

Night vision in CCTV offers clarity, making it ideal for low-light areas and during the night. If areas have dimmed lighting, you may not benefit from the night vision feature; instead, you may need a CCTV camera with low light performance and a wide aperture, allowing the camera to absorb more light from dimly-lit areas.

Frames Per Second (FPS)

The frames per second is the number of images that occur in one second. The higher the frames per second selected, the clearer the footage will be. You can select from 1 to 30 frames per second, sometimes even 60. It is not necessarily a good idea to record at a high frame per second as it would take up more storage capacity and reduce internet speed. 15 FPS is typically sufficient for clear footage.

What You Need to Know Before
Purchasing a Keyless Card Access System

What is a Keyless Card Access System and How Does It Work?

A Keyless Card Access System is a form of security that controls, manages, and monitors your employees and visitors, giving them access to an area at any given time while keeping track of who enters. This system can keep your employees, premises, and inventory safe. Individuals would receive their credentials either in the form of cards, fobs, fingerprints or on a mobile device, identifying a person seeking access. The electrically-powered doors are typically locked 24/7 and only grant access to authorized personnel for a short period when a badge is swiped, and their credentials are verified. Meanwhile, the system restricts access to unauthorized personnel. Access would be granted by an access control panel, sending the door lock a signal to unlock.

What is the Purpose of a Keyless Card Access System and What Are its Benefits?

A Card Access System allows you to control, manage and monitor who enters your premises while adding a layer of security compared to traditional locks and keys. One of the many benefits of installing a keyless card access system is that if your employee loses a key or leaves your company, you will no longer need to change your locks or even ask for the key back. You would log on to your online portal and deactivate the user, saving you money in the long run.

Cards, instead of keys, are much more challenging to duplicate, preventing employees from copying them. Manual locks can be picked by intruders, whereas with an electronic card access system, you would have to rip apart the access strip from the door to gain entry.

What is Needed for a Keyless Card Access System to Work?

For an Access Control System to work, your door will need to be electrified, electronically unlocking your door when a badge is swiped. It is done by installing an electric or magnetic lock, the most popular methods. An electric door strike is installed in the door frame and acts as a latch; when energized, the latch will open. This is the cheapest of the two-door locks and the most common. Electric strikes are usually "fail secure," meaning that your door would stay locked in the event of a power outage. Electric strikes are usually installed on wood-framed and metal doors. Electric strikes allow a person inside to push the release bar to exit even when the strike is in the closed position.

Another common lock sometimes used with an Access Control System is Maglocks, which contains two pieces of metal: one metal plate mounted on the door and the other piece on the door frame. When powered, a Maglock uses electromagnetic force to stop doors from opening. Maglocks are usually fail-safe so that they will release and open for people in the event of a power failure. A double-door or glass door with no center post cannot be controlled with a strike, so they would need a Maglock as a strong locking force. A power supply with a backup battery is commonly installed to provide emergency power to magnetic locks. Another form of lock is an electrified push bar that is used to comply with fire codes.

Component Parts of a Keyless Card Access System

Software portal/ mobile app: A Card Access System typically comes with a portal, whether onsite or cloud-based. It is a manageable dashboard through which the admin can access, control, and manage door entries. Card Access Portals allow the admin to:

- Enable/ disable / manage doors
- Control and manage users
- Set time schedules for employees to have access
- Customize the system to send texts and email notifications for designated events
- Control multiple facilities/ locations all in one portal (if you have a cloud-based system)
- Unlock doors remotely
- And more!

Onsite Card Access System vs. Cloud-Based Card Access System

An Onsite Card Access System usually requires the software to be on a shared or separate PC on site, making it difficult to control the system remotely. On the other hand, a Cloud-Based Card Access System stores all access permissions on the cloud (internet) as opposed to a local server, allowing you to pull up your portal from any computer or mobile device anywhere in the world with internet connectivity to control and manage your system from outside. In addition to an online portal, Card Access Systems typically come with a mobile app to control the system and sometimes to unlock doors remotely.

Card reader: A card reader is usually mounted outside your door for users to swipe, verifying their credentials to grant access. A Card Access Control System has different readers or devices that grant access. Some readers use biometrics that allows access to users who press their thumbs for prints. Some readers contain built-in numeric keypads for users to enter a pin code for access instead of swiping a card or key fob. Some systems allow you to gain entry with a button on a mobile device. Bluetooth readers can grant users access when standing near the reader and sometimes work if you do not have an internet connection on-premises.

Proximity Cards

A proximity card is a physical card used to grant access. Proxy cards contain several thousand copper wires and, if tampered with, would stop working.

Key Fobs

A plastic security token disc like a size of a poker chip containing internal technology.

Biometric

While they are more expensive, fingerprints, palm prints, and facial recognition are other methods used by an Access Control System to verify identity and grant access.

Mobile App

Mobile app access also exists in the card access world. Instead of carrying a card or key fob, users can gain access by holding their phone near the reader or pressing a button on their phone app.

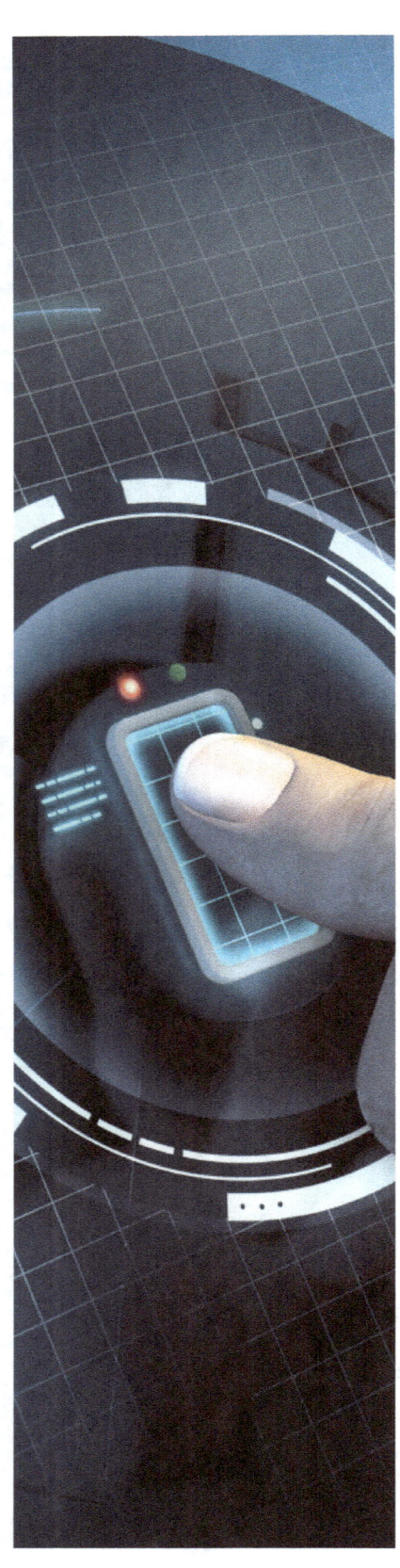

Control Panel:

The access control panel is the system's brain and is usually installed in a server or IT room. Your card access wires and locks are wired to it. When a credential is presented, the panel receives the request to unlock and then unlocks the door. The panel stores and records all permissions and events regarding access, which can be pulled by the admin later. The server can use Windows, Linux, or a cloud-based server.

Power Supply

Card Access Systems come with a 12, 16, or 24 Volt AC & DC Transformer, a power supply, and a backup battery in different shapes and sizes.

Request to Exit/Egress Buttons

A button or motion sensor installed inside a room to detect people leaving, allowing them to exit freely and safely as quickly as possible. This is sometimes required to meet life safety codes.

Cables

Typical gauges used for Card Access Systems are 24, 22, 18, and 16 AWG sizes, the most common being the 18:2 gauge. A CAT6 cable is typically connected from the readers/ controllers to the internet router or switch. Power is also needed for the door lock and control panel.

What You Need to Know Before Purchasing an Intercom System

What is a Door Intercom System?

A Door Intercom (Intercommunication) System provides two-way communication with a visitor outside a secured door and grants them access with the press of a button from your indoor station or remotely. The visitor outside will ring your outdoor station to announce themselves. You would then identify the guest by communicating via voice and sometimes view them on video on the indoor master within the building or a cell phone app remotely.

If you choose to grant them access, you will press a button on your indoor master, substation, or mobile app, whether it be on your cellphone or tablet. An intercom system comes with either audio-only or audio and video. Some Door Intercom Systems cannot unlock doors; instead only provide two-way communication via voice and sometimes video.

Types of Intercoms

Wired Intercom Systems: Generally speaking, it is best to install a wired intercom system as opposed to a wireless system as wired systems are more dependable and do not interfere with neighboring systems like wireless systems sometimes do. Furthermore, they last longer and require less maintenance. Voice, picture, and communication quality should be clearer on a wired intercom system than on a wireless one. Wired intercom systems can use cat 5/6 network cables or two-wire shielded cables.

Wireless Intercom Systems

When running wires is impossible or too difficult, a wireless system can be used. Wireless Intercom Systems use radio signals to communicate between outdoor and indoor stations. One pro of installing a wireless system is that no wires need to be run between the two stations, providing a much easier installation. They are also cheaper. The cons are that they generally have a lesser picture and voice quality than a wired system. They have less range and may not even work if installed in a building with a lot of concrete and metal or if the outdoor station is too far from the indoor station. Other neighboring systems can also sometimes tune into your frequency. Wireless intercom systems are usually best suited for smaller businesses and homes.

Video Intercom Systems

Video Intercom Systems include a camera in the outside station and an internal monitor for the user to see who is outside seeking to gain entry. These systems come with a speaker and a push button. Most Video Intercom cameras are of moderate quality and have fixed viewing angles. Video can also be viewed from a mobile app remotely.

Apartment Intercom Systems

An Apartment Intercom System allows guests to dial into the apartment unit they desire. The tenants in the building would be able to communicate with their guests and provide access with a click of a button. This system would require an outdoor station outside the building and an indoor station in each unit.

IP Network Connected Intercoms

A new development in intercoms is IP network-connected intercom stations that can be plugged into your data network, allowing you to bridge two or more intercom systems located in separate buildings of the same facility over an existing Internet, LAN, or WAN network. This setup allows single communication for all employees. It would also reduce the labor and cost of installing wiring. A cat5/6 network cable would need to run to each IP Intercom System. IP Intercoms typically come with a mobile app through which calls can be forwarded if no one answers from inside the facility. This would allow you to see who is outside, communicate with them, and buzz them in - all remotely from your mobile app or computer.

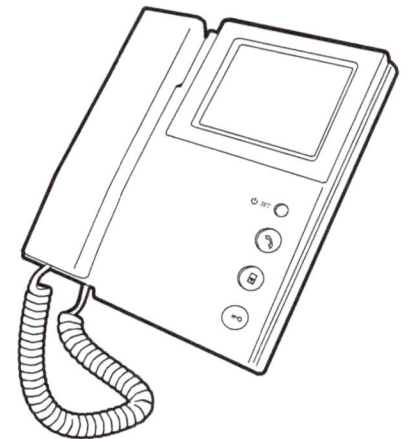

Components of an Intercom System

Outdoor Station: The Outdoor Intercom Station allows your guest or delivery person outside to alert you via your indoor Master Station that someone is outside. Your guest can communicate with you inside via your indoor station's microphone/ speaker. You can view and verify who is outside by looking at the camera if the station has one. You can install multiple outdoor stations within a business or home if you have more than one entry point.

Indoor Master Station

The Master Indoor Station allows you to communicate with your visitor outside with the talk button. The guest can be buzzed in with a press of a button. It comes with a speaker, volume control, and sometimes a monitor to view who is outside.

Indoor Substation

The Indoor Sub-Master Station is connected with your Master Station and provides a similar capability. A Sub-Master is used when visitor verification and buzzing are required from multiple areas within a business or home. You can install multiple indoor stations within a business or home.

Intercom Mobile App and Computer Software

Your Intercom Mobile App allows you to monitor and buzz guests while it forwards intercom calls to you by means of a mobile app on your phone, tablet, or even a computer via software (if your intercom system contains that feature). Many systems have a sliding button on their app to prevent accidental clicking that would unlock a door. You can customize your system to receive notifications and view recorded calls and clips of missed calls.

What You Need to Know Before Purchasing Cyber Security

What is Cyber Security?

Cyber security, also known as network security, protects your organization's digital infrastructure, including your networks, computers, servers, data, computer software, and emails, from unauthorized outside harm. Such harm comes in the form of changing, destroying, spying, or stealing anything in your organization's digital infrastructure.

Why Do you Need Cyber Security?

With the rapid growth of technology and its use in organizations today, protecting your network has become critical. More hackers are attacking people and businesses across the globe and are savvier and more inventive than ever.

A cyber-attack occurs every thirty seconds. Cyber-attack damage is projected to exceed $6 trillion by 2021, encouraging more and more companies to invest in cybersecurity to protect their businesses, networks, and data. On average, a cyber-attack incident costs a small business roughly $250,000 to fix and fully recover from the breach, resulting in 60% of companies closing within six months due to a lack of capital to overcome the attack.

It becomes imperative for any organization to prepare now to prevent attacks that can lead to severe consequences, especially with many businesses transmitting sensitive data across networks and people working from home or outside their offices.

Who is Vulnerable to an Attack?

All small, medium, and large businesses are vulnerable to cyber-attacks. About half of these attacks last year targeted victims of small businesses.

What are the Different Forms of Cyber Threats?

Malware

Malware (malicious software) is an umbrella term for harmful software designed to damage or steal information from a computer or network. Malware can include computer viruses, while ransomware is spread via an email attachment or a clicked link.

Ransomware

Ransomware is a form of malware that encrypts or locks your program or files so that you lose access unless you pay the hacker. Payment will often unlock it or provide the required decryption key to restore access in Bitcoin or other cryptocurrencies. Ransomware is usually delivered through phishing emails and exploits any software vulnerabilities.

Phishing Emails

Phishing emails are very common and usually sent to you and your employees to trick them into clicking a link or opening an email attachment; but it contains malicious code to surrender the user's credentials. These emails are typically disguised to look legitimate as if they are coming from an employee, your business, bank, or someone you know. These emails use your organization's same business names, logos, wording, etc., to appear more legitimate and fool employees. Once a phishing link is clicked, cybercriminals access sensitive data like credit cards, social security, or login information. They usually ask you to reset your password so it would be visible to the hacker. Some phishing emails are sent to thousands of people simultaneously, while others are specially crafted for specific, vulnerable targets.

Spear-Phishing

Spear-Phishing is a type of phishing email disguised to appear like an email sent from someone you know and trust personally, like your boss or an executive from your company. The purpose is to entice you to reveal confidential information or enter your password.

Virus, Trojans, and Worms

While these three terms are often used interchangeably, they are not the same. While viruses, worms, and Trojan Horses are all malicious programs that can cause damage to a computer, knowing the difference should help you better protect your computer.

Virus

A virus is a computer program or type of software that connects itself to another software program to harm your computer. When you run the software with the virus attached, it spreads from one computer to another, leaving infections as it travels. It spreads like a human virus and cannot be controlled remotely.

Trojan Horse

A Trojan Horse is a harmful piece of software disguised to look like legitimate software to trick you into downloading it to your computer. A Trojan Horse does not replicate itself like a computer virus and worm; instead, it is hidden in a piece of code that can steal, delete, or modify your data. For example, Trojan Horse software can observe your email username and password when logging on to your email on the Web.

Worms

A computer worm is like a computer virus, as it can replicate itself and cause damage; but unlike a computer virus, it does not require a host program or someone to open it to infect. A worm enters a computer through a vulnerability in your system and takes advantage of a file or information transport.

Spyware

Unlike a virus, spyware does not replicate itself, but it can secretly collect sensitive information, such as financial data, credit card numbers, passwords, etc. Most likely, you will never even notice it was there.

Cyber Security Facts

- A cyber-attack occurs roughly every 30-seconds.

- It costs a small business roughly $250,000 to fix and recover from a cyber-attack.

- 60% of small businesses that get attacked go out of business within six months.

- About 90% of cyber-attacks start with a phishing campaign asking an employee to click a link or download an attachment.

- About half of the cyber-attacks last year were on small businesses.

- Businesses lost roughly 30% of their annual revenue from cyber-attacks.

- About 65% of malicious software is installed via a malicious email attachment.

- About 60% of phishing emails contain ransomware.

- Retail anti-virus software installed on your computer alone is not enough to protect your computer and network

What Can Cyber Security Do for You and How Would it Protect Your Business?

Cyber security ensures that only authorized employees have access to your business data, whether working in the office, a café, or remotely from home. A cybersecurity setup would include multiple layers of protection from outside threats across your entire digital infrastructure - from your networks and computers to software, emails, etc.

A Cyber Security Solution Offers:

- 24/7 real-time threat protection, inspecting every bit of data coming in, no matter the source— even encrypted traffic.

- Installed firewall to protect against outside threats by inspecting all incoming network traffic.

- Anti-virus and anti-spyware to prevent malicious software from entering.

- A content-filtering service, allowing you to control and manage the sites your employees visit.

- An online portal and performance report.

- An email filtering service to prevent phishing emails from being sent to your employees' email inbox by inspecting emails and filtering out emails with threats.

- VPN that helps protect your network when you are working remotely.

- Affordable protection

Visit www.everythingsecuritysystems.com to request a security advisor contact you with information and pricing on how to protect your family, business, and assets!

Everything Security
S Y S T E M S